W9-BEC-575

Date: 2/12/15

J 641.5123 SCH
Schuette, Sarah L.,
A superhero cookbook : simple
recipes for kids /

PALM BEACH COUNTY
LIBRARY SYSTEM
3650 SUMMIT BLVD.
WEST PALM BEACH, FL 33406

First Facts

First Cookbooks

A Superhero
COOKBOOK

Simple Recipes for Kids

by Sarah L. Schuette

CAPSTONE PRESS
a capstone imprint

First Facts is published by Capstone Press,
1710 Roe Crest Drive, North Mankato, Minnesota 56003.
www.capstonepub.com

Copyright © 2012 by Capstone Press, a Capstone imprint.
All rights reserved.
No part of this publication may be reproduced in whole or in part, or stored in a
retrieval system, or transmitted in any form or by any means, electronic, mechanical, photocopying,
recording, or otherwise, without written permission of the publisher.
For information regarding permission, write to Capstone Press,
1710 Roe Crest Drive, North Mankato, Minnesota 56003.

 Books published by Capstone Press are manufactured with paper
containing at least 10 percent post-consumer waste.

Library of Congress Cataloging-in-Publication Data
Schuette, Sarah L., 1976–
  A superhero cookbook : simple recipes for kids / by Sarah L. Schuette.
    p. cm.—(First facts. First cookbooks)
  Includes bibliographical references and index.
  Summary: "Provides instructions and step-by-step photos for making a variety of simple snacks and drinks
with a superhero theme"—Provided by publisher.
  ISBN 978-1-4296-5998-7 (library binding)
  1. Cooking—Juvenile literature. 2. Quick and easy cooking—Juvenile literature. 3. Snack foods—Juvenile
literature. 4. Cookbooks—Juvenile literature. 5. Superheroes—Juvenile literature. I. Title. II. Series.

  TX652.5.S344 2012
  641.5'55—dc22   2011001804

Editorial Credits
Christine Peterson, editor; Heidi Thompson, designer; Sarah Schuette, photo stylist; Marcy Morin, studio
      scheduler; Laura Manthe, production specialist

Photo Credits
All images Capstone Studio/Karon Dubke except:
iStockphoto/Bill Noll, sparkle design

The author dedicates this book in memory of her aunt, Ruthy Hilgers, a real superhero in her life.

Printed in the United States of America in North Mankato, Minnesota.
122012
007090R

Table of Contents

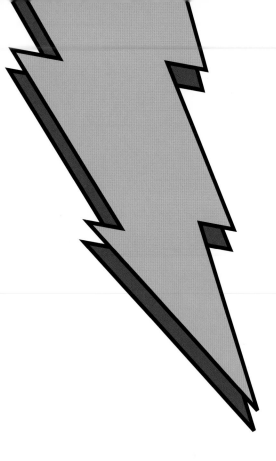

Super Cooks!

Kapow! Zwoosh! Blam! Superheroes save the day with their superpowers. You can be a superhero in the kitchen. No super strength required. Just zoom into the kitchen and get cooking!

Look over each recipe with your **X-ray vision**. Then use your super brain waves to find the tools and **ingredients** you need. Hit a **force field**? Ask an adult for help.

Turn that cape around, and use it for an apron. Zip over to the sink, and wash your hands. When you're finished, hit the mess with an eraser blast. Superheroes always keep their kitchens clean.

Metric Conversion Chart	
United States	**Metric**
¼ teaspoon	1.2 mL
½ teaspoon	2.5 mL
1 teaspoon	5 mL
1 tablespoon	15 mL
¼ cup	60 mL
⅓ cup	80 mL
½ cup	120 mL
⅔ cup	160 mL
¾ cup	175 mL
1 cup	240 mL
1 ounce	30 gms

Tools

The kitchen is the source of your superpowers. Everything you'll need is right at your fingertips. Use this guide to pick the right stuff.

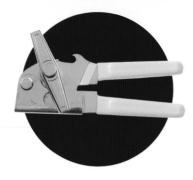

can opener—a tool used to open metal cans

citrus squeezer—a small tool used to get juice from fruit

cutting board—a wooden or plastic board used when slicing or chopping foods

egg slicer—a small tool with wires used for slicing eggs

liquid measuring cup—a glass or plastic measuring cup with a spout for pouring

measuring cups—round cups with handles used for measuring dry ingredients

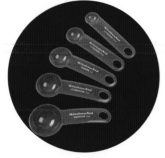

measuring spoons—spoons with small deep scoops used to measure both wet and dry ingredients

mixing bowl—a sturdy bowl used for mixing ingredients

muffin pan—a pan with individual cups for baking muffins or cupcakes

drain—to remove the liquid from something

drizzle—to let a liquid fall in small drops

measure—to take a specific amount of something

stir—to mix something by moving a spoon around in it

toss—to mix gently with two spoons or forks

oven mitt—a large mitten made from heavy fabric used to protect hands when removing hot pans from the oven

skewer—a long, thin stick used to hold food

strainer—a bowl-shaped tool with holes in the sides and bottom used for draining liquid off food

Captain Egg Heads

Stomach grumbling? Let Captain Egg Head punch your hunger with a **protein** blast. You'll have the energy to fight crime all day long.

Makes 6

Ingredients:
- 1 hard-boiled egg
- round crackers
- shredded carrots
- shredded cheese
- black olive slices
- bacon bits
- chives

Tools:
- cutting board
- egg slicer
- plate

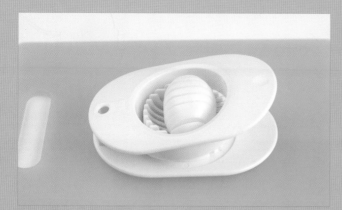

1 On a cutting board, use an egg slicer to cut the egg.

2 Place a cracker on a plate. Top cracker with a slice of egg.

3 Decorate cracker to look like your favorite superhero. Add shredded carrots or cheese for hair. Olives or bacon bits can be eyes. Chives make great eyebrows.

4 Repeat with more crackers until you have your own team of superheroes.

TIP:
No need to cook your own eggs. You can find hard-boiled eggs at the supermarket.

Gamma Rays

Zap! Turn plain sandwich ingredients into **gamma rays** of goodness. Better hurry. These snacks will be gone in a flash.

Makes 1

Ingredients:
- 1 whole-wheat bun
- cheese cubes
- ham cubes
- cherry tomatoes
- pickle slices
- fat-free ranch dressing for dipping

Tools:
- butter knife
- cutting board
- 1 skewer

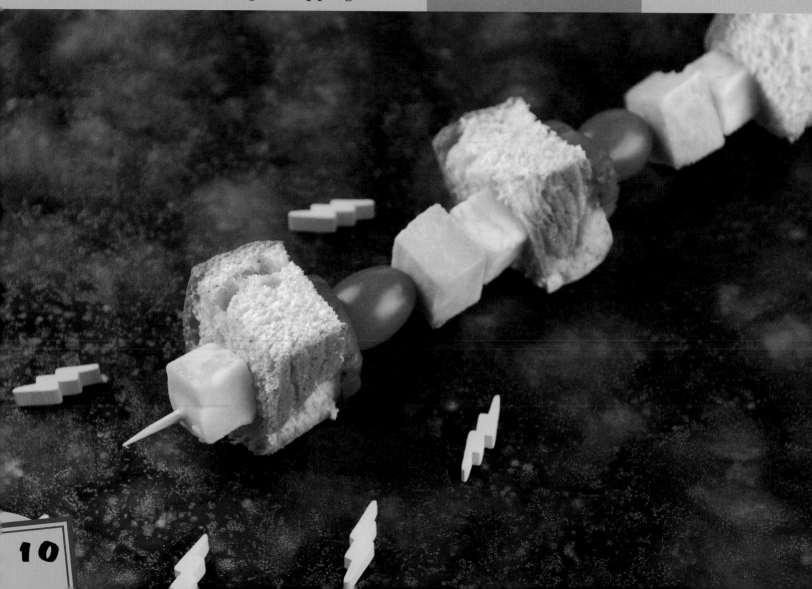

1 With an adult's help, cut bun into cubes on a cutting board.

2 Slide one bread cube onto a skewer.

3 Next, slide a piece of cheese on the skewer.

4 Add ham, tomato, pickle, and another bread cube to skewer.

5 Add more ingredients until skewer is full. Dip pieces into ranch dressing as you eat.

Super-Powered Salsa

Villains got you down? Let Super Salsa Girl come to your rescue! One bite of her sweet salsa will turn any **foe** into a friend.

Makes 1 serving

Ingredients:
- 1 tablespoon brown sugar
- 2 tablespoons apple jelly
- 2 fruit cups, any kind
- 2 strawberries, chopped
- 12 raspberries
- pita chips

Tools:
- mixing bowl
- measuring spoons
- spoon
- strainer
- knife
- cutting board

1 In a mixing bowl, measure and add brown sugar and apple jelly. Stir to combine.

2 Using a strainer, drain juice from fruit cups. Add fruit to bowl.

3 Have an adult help you cut strawberries on a cutting board. Add strawberry pieces to the bowl.

4 Add raspberries to bowl. Mix fruit together.

5 Serve salsa with pita chips.

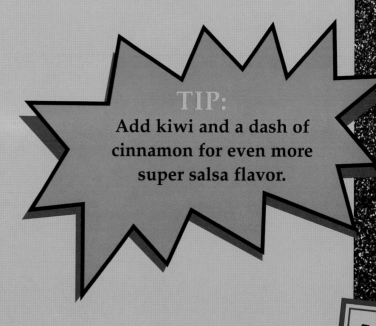

TIP:
Add kiwi and a dash of cinnamon for even more super salsa flavor.

Salad Man Saves the Day

Are your cupboards empty? Refrigerator bare?
Call on Salad Man. He'll be there. With one look,
he makes a salad appear.

Ingredients:

- ½ cup fat-free mayonnaise
- 1 tablespoon lemon juice
- 1 tablespoon brown sugar
- 1 tablespoon soy sauce
- 1 tablespoon vinegar
- 1 bag baby spinach, washed
- 1 9.75-ounce can chunk chicken
- 1 12-ounce can mandarin oranges
- 2 cups chow mein noodles
- ½ cup slivered almonds (optional)

Tools:

- empty jar with lid
- measuring cups
- measuring spoons
- large bowl
- can opener
- strainer
- 2 spoons

1 In an empty jar with lid, measure and add mayo.

2 Measure and add lemon juice, brown sugar, soy sauce, and vinegar. Close jar and shake to combine. Set aside.

3 Add washed spinach to a large bowl.

4 Open can, and use a strainer to drain liquid from chicken. Add chicken to bowl.

5 Open mandarin oranges. Drain liquid, and add oranges to bowl.

6 Measure and add noodles and almonds. Drizzle dressing over salad. Toss ingredients to coat.

Crime-Fighting Carrots

Is your night vision a little dim? Can't see through walls as usual? Check out this tasty dish. Your X-ray vision will improve with your first bite.

Ingredients:
- 1 15-ounce can sliced, cooked carrots
- 2 tablespoons butter
- 1 tablespoon dry ranch dressing mix
- 2 tablespoons brown sugar

Tools:
- can opener
- strainer
- microwave-safe bowl
- measuring spoons
- oven mitts
- spoon
- plastic wrap

1 Using a can opener, open carrots. Drain with a strainer.

2 In a microwave-safe bowl, measure and add butter, dressing mix, and brown sugar.

3 With an adult's help, melt butter mixture in the microwave for about 15 seconds.

4 With oven mitts, remove bowl from microwave. Mix ingredients together.

5 Add carrots to bowl and stir.

6 Cover bowl with plastic wrap. Microwave for 1 minute.

Muscle Bars

Even superheroes need to eat breakfast. Fuel up with these cereal bars. They're a power-packed snack for crime-fighters on the go. Stuff a few in your cape's pocket for munching any time of day.

Makes 12 bars

Ingredients:
- 1 cup dried cranberries
- 1 cup almonds
- 1 cup chocolate chips
- 1 cup toasted oat cereal
- ½ stick butter
- 1 10-ounce bag marshmallows

Tools:
- measuring cups
- 2 large bowls
- spoon
- microwave-safe bowl
- muffin pan
- non-stick cooking spray

1 Measure and add cranberries, almonds, chocolate chips, and cereal into a large bowl. Mix with spoon. Set aside.

2 In a microwave-safe bowl, measure and add butter and marshmallows. Microwave for two minutes.

3 Have an adult take bowl out of microwave with oven mitts and stir mixture.

4 Pour cereal mixture into marshmallows and stir.

5 Spray muffin pan with cooking spray.

6 With a spoon, fill each muffin cup with the mixture. Press down. Let cool for 10 minutes before eating.

ZAM! POW! Punch

Busy day? Use your time-stopping power to take a break. Smack your taste buds with a super **citrus** punch. You'll be back in action and ready for the next adventure.

Ingredients:

- ½ cup lemon-lime soda
- ice cubes
- 2 limes
- 1 teaspoon cherry juice
- 1 cherry

Tools:

- tall glass
- liquid measuring cup
- knife
- cutting board
- citrus squeezer
- measuring spoons
- spoon

1 In a tall glass, measure and pour soda over ice cubes.

2 With an adult's help, cut the limes in half on a cutting board.

3 Squeeze the limes with a citrus squeezer. Pour juice into glass.

4 Measure cherry juice and add to glass.

5 Stir well with a spoon. Top punch with one cherry.

Glossary

citrus (SIT-ruhss)—a juicy fruit such as a lemon, lime, orange, or grapefruit

foe (FOH)—an enemy

force field (FORS FEELD)—a wall made of energy that stops movement

gamma ray (GAM-muh RAY)—a ray that is like an X-ray but has more energy

ingredient (in-GREE-dee-uhnt)—an item used to make something else

protein (PROH-teen)—a substance found in foods such as meat, cheese, eggs, and fish

villain (VIL-uhn)—a wicked, evil, or bad person who is often a character in a story

X-ray vision (EKS-ray VIZH-uhn)—the ability to see inside a person or through objects

Read More

Fauchald, Nick. *Holy Guacamole!: and Other Scrumptious Snacks.* Kids Dish. Minneapolis: Picture Window Books, 2008.

Grant, Amanda. *Grow It, Cook It with Kids.* New York: Ryland Peters & Small, 2010.

Internet Sites

FactHound offers a safe, fun way to find Internet sites related to this book. All of the sites on FactHound have been researched by our staff.

Here's all you do:

Visit *www.facthound.com*

Type in this code: 9781429659987

Super-cool stuff!

Check out projects, games and lots more at
www.capstonekids.com

Index